Please renew or return items by the date shown on your receipt

www.hertsdirect.org/libraries

| Renewals and enquiries: | 0300 123 4049 |
| Textphone for hearing or speech impaired | 0300 123 4041 |

Hertfordshire

Prince Philip: Wise Words and Golden Gaffes

Published by
Barzipan Publishing
www.barzipan.com

ISBN 978-0-9573792-2-0
ePub edition ISBN 978-0-9573792-3-7

Printed and bound by Short Run Press, Exeter

CIP Data: A catalogue record for this book is available from the British Library.

Prince Philip
Wise Words and Golden Gaffes

Phil Dampier &
Ashley Walton

with illustrations by Richard Jolley

Barzipan Publishing
not what you'd expect

PHIL DAMPIER has been writing about the royal family for 26 years.

Between 1986 and 1991 he covered the royal beat for *The Sun*, Britain's biggest-selling daily newspaper.

As a freelance journalist for the last 20 years, he has travelled to more than 50 countries, following members of the House of Windsor, and his articles have been published in dozens of newspapers and magazines worldwide. He frequently appears on radio and TV, and gave expert analysis for Global National TV of Canada during their coverage of the wedding of the Duke and Duchess of Cambridge in April 2011.

He lives in Kent with his partner Ann.

ASHLEY WALTON was the royal correspondent of the *Daily Express* from 1979 to 1992.

He travelled to every continent covering numerous tours, including the Queen and Prince Philip in India, Africa and China.

He was one of the first reporters to identify a young Lady Diana Spencer as a future royal bride, and covered her last tour with Prince Charles to South Korea in 1992. He was also among the first to reveal the romance between Prince Andrew and Sarah Ferguson.

He lives in Hertfordshire with his wife Joan. They have two adult sons.

RICHARD JOLLEY has been a freelance cartoonist for twenty years. He has contributed to many national newspapers and regularly appears in *Private Eye*, *The Spectator* and the *Mail On Sunday*. He drew the strip 'Liz' about the Royals in Private Eye. His work has been exhibited in the National Portrait Gallery, Victoria and Albert Museum and the Cartoon Museum.

Born in Lancashire, raised in Cheshire, he lives in North London with his wife and two children.

CONTENTS

SOURCES & ACKNOWLEDGEMENTS

Some of these 'gaffes' and comments were witnessed by the authors. Many have come from hours of combing through national and local newspaper reports. We are also grateful for material from the following sources:

Books

Butler, Peter, *The Wit of Prince Philip*. Leslie Frewin, London, 1965

HRH Duke of Edinburgh, *Men, Machines and Sacred Cows*. Hamish Hamilton, London, 1984

Prince Philip Speaks: Selected Speeches 1956-59. Collins, London.

Brandreth, Gyles, *Philip and Elizabeth – Portrait of a Marriage*. Century, London, 2004

Interviews

A Strange Life: Profile of Prince Philip by Fiammetta Rocco. *Independent on Sunday*. December 1992

'I've just got to live with it.' Interview by Gyles Brandreth. *Sunday Telegraph*. May 1999

Duke takes the hazards in stride. Interview by Sue Mott. *Daily Telegraph*. May 2006

TV Programmes

The Duke: A Portrait of Prince Philip with Sir Trevor McDonald. ITV 2008

Prince Philip at 90 with Alan Titchmarsh. ITV 2011

The Duke at 90 with Fiona Bruce. BBC 2011

INTRODUCTION

When *Duke of Hazard The Wit and Wisdom of Prince Philip* was first published in 2006 to mark his 85th birthday, it received worldwide publicity and critical acclaim.

Even though some of his comments must have been lost in translation, newspapers, magazines, radio and TV stations from as far afield as Colombia, Bahrain and Poland quoted from the book, which instantly became a best-seller.

Perhaps he struck a global chord as a free-thinking individual, refusing to conform or change his views for the sake of others.

He can be controversial, irascible, and sometimes downright rude. But would we have had it any other way?

Five years on he celebrated his 90th birthday in 2011 with several parties, and tributes poured in from politicians, the public and members of his own family.

The 'Iron Duke' was taken to hospital at Christmas in 2011 with a heart condition, and missed some of the Diamond Jubilee celebrations in 2012 with a bladder infection. But at 91, he is still determined to live a full life and support the Queen in every way he can.

In *Prince Philip: Wise Words and Golden Gaffes* we have attempted to highlight not only Philip's wit, but also plenty of his wisdom too. Way ahead of his time on many issues, his views on the environment, over-population, religion, politics and the press are as relevant today as those of many public figures half his age.

So, once again, enjoy the unique style of this national treasure, whose down to earth humour and no-nonsense approach have brought so much colour and vitality into our lives.

At home and abroad, no-one is safe when the 'Gaffer', the Prince of political incorrectness, gets going.

Much to our relief, Philip has continued to make headlines in the last few years with his quirky humour and forthright views.

Here in this bang up to date edition and in no particular order, are his latest quips, along with the best from previous decades.

THE PRINCE OF POLITICAL INCORRECTNESS

Just a month after his 85th birthday, Philip proved he was going to carry on dishing it out as normal.

While giving out Duke of Edinburgh Award Scheme prizes at Holyroodhouse in Scotland, a student told him he had been working in Romania.

'Romania?' Philip asked. *'You didn't go across to help in one of those orphanages did you?'*

When the student said No, the Prince exclaimed, *'Ah, good, there's so many of those orphanages over there you feel they breed them just to put them in orphanages.'*

(2006)

At a Buckingham Palace reception to thank those involved in the Diamond Jubilee celebrations, Prince Philip met Conservative Health Secretary Jeremy Hunt.

'Who are you?' he asked.

Hunt explained he was Health Secretary but had been Culture Secretary during the Jubilee and Olympics.

'Well they do move you people on a lot,' said Philip, walking off.

(2012)

At a lunch at the Palace, Philip was seated next to Poirot star David Suchet. Each was presented with a whole mango for a pudding. Turning to the Duke the actor asked advice on peeling the fruit.

'You don't peel a mango, you slice it!' was the curt reply as Philip grabbed sharp knife and demonstrated.

(2012)

On a walkabout in Bromley, Kent, he spotted 90-year-old Barbara Dubery sitting in a wheelchair, wrapped in a foil blanket to fend off the cold.

'Are they going to put you in the oven next?' asked Philip.

(2012)

The same day, he was confronted by pretty, 25-year-old blonde, Hannah Jackson, in a red dress with a zip down the front. Philip turned to a nearby policeman and said:

'I would get arrested if I unzipped that dress!'

(2012)

To Stoke-on-Trent MP Joan Walley at a reception:

'Where do you represent?'

'Stoke,' she replied.

'Ghastly place, isn't it?' said Philip

(1997)

In Lambeth Palace he chanced upon a corner full of women, including a nun and the Rev Canon Dr Frances Ward, the Dean of St Edmundsbury Cathedral.

Flinging his arms out wide he declared:

'So this is the female section. Are you all gathered here for protection?'

(2012)

After glancing at business chief Atul Patel's name badge during a Palace reception for 400 influential British Indians:

'There's a lot of your family in tonight!'

(2009)

On a visit to Manchester he chatted to students at the University of Salford and said:

'Do you fight?'

When he was introduced to one local and one student from Sheffield he asked:

'Do you understand each other?'

(2012)

To Buckingham Palace garden party guest Stephen Judge, who was sporting a small 'patch' beard:

'What do you do?'

'I'm a designer, Sir.'

'Well you're obviously not a hirsute designer!'

Seeing Stephen's flustered expression, Philip added, *'Your beard man – your poor, frustrated beard! If you're going to grow a beard, grow a beard! You really must try harder.'*

(2009)

At the opening ceremony of the Commonwealth Heads of Government meeting in Perth, Australia he watched a troupe of Aborigines cavort in traditional costume and said:

'You won't see that in the Outback!'

(2012)

The bystander looked affronted, assuming that the Duke was accusing him of being a drunk, and the witticism fell rather flat. It should be explained that the Soke of Peterborough was a county in its own right – a historical anachronism – until it was abolished in 1965. That was the only time that the Royal Maundy was distributed in Peterborough.

(1975)

After being told that Madonna was singing the *Die Another Day* theme at the film's world premiere in the Albert Hall he asked her:

'Are we going to need ear plugs?'

(2002)

You're just a silly little Whitehall twit – you don't trust me and I don't trust you.'

To Sir Rennie Maudslay, Keeper of the Privy Purse in the 1970s.

(2002)

On a visit to the Wyvern Barracks in Exeter he asked 24-year-old sea cadet Elizabeth Rendle what she did.

Told she worked in a night club he asked: *'Do you work in a strip club?'*

And then added, *'I suppose it's probably too cold for that anyway.'*

(2010)

To disabled mobility scooter rider David Miller, 60:

'How many people have you knocked over this morning on that thing?'

Later the same day in Waltham Forest, London, he asked mayor Geoff Walker, who has cerebral palsy and problems with walking:

'Have you run over anybody?'

(2012)

To ex-pats in Abu Dhabi:

'Are you running away from something?'

(2010)

Addressing multi-ethnic *Britain's Got Talent* winners Diversity, who are from London, after a performance at the Royal Variety Show:

'Are you all one family?'

'Did you all come over just for this one show?'

(2009)

To Paraguay dictator General Alfredo Stroessner:

'It's a pleasure to be in a country that isn't ruled by its people.'

(1963)

In the early days of his marriage Philip would often try to lighten up formal occasions.

At glittering Buckingham Palace banquets he would pick up the gold-embossed menu written in French and say:

'Oh good – fish and chips again!'

At a Buckingham Palace reception for the 50th anniversary of the Duke of Edinburgh Awards, he said:

'We get a small government grant, and I sometimes wonder, why bother?

'You sell your soul to the government and that's it.'

(2006)

'The best thing to do with a degree is to forget it.'

At Salford University.

When Harold Newman of the Association of Jewish Ex-Servicemen reminded Philip that on a previous visit he had described his members as 'taxi drivers and clothing manufacturers' the Duke replied:

'No, I said they were taxi drivers and tailors.'

(2007)

To a school band in Cairns, Australia:

'You were playing your instruments weren't you? Or do you have tape recorders under your seats?'

(2002)

To actor Simon Pegg after the London premiere of the *Chronicles of Narnia:*

'When did you first realise you had the voice of a mouse?'

(2008)

To disabled comedian Adam Hills, who has a prosthetic limb:

'You could smuggle a bottle of gin out of the country in that artificial foot.'

(2009)

Showing benefactors of Cambridge University around Windsor Castle, he guided them into the grand Waterloo Chamber, built to commemorate Wellington's victory in 1815.

And if you happen to be French, it's the music room,' quipped Philip.

(2010)

At his 70th birthday party in Windsor Castle he met Terrie Doherty, then head of Sony Music Regional Promotion in London.

'What do you do?' he asked.

Told that he had to deal with radio and TV producers, the Duke said:

'God! Do you have to speak to those awful DJ chappies?'

(1991)

On a visit to Swansea he met four local belly dancers and told them:

'I thought Eastern women just sat around smoking pipes and eating sweets all day.'

(2008)

Shown some Ethiopian art:

'It looks like the kind of thing my daughter would bring back from school art lessons.'

(1965)

At a medieval fayre in Old Windsor, a lady in period costume was breast-feeding her baby in a quiet corner.

The Duke spotted her and said loudly:

'What are you doing m'lady?'

There was an embarrassed silence before he added:

'Oh look everyone, she's really taken the part to heart and is breast-feeding her child!'

On a visit to Crawley with the Queen to celebrate the town's 60th anniversary, Philip wandered into the Druckers Vienna Patisserie. He pointed to a display of cream cakes and asked manager Claire Burns:

'Are you responsible for making people overweight in Crawley?'

Claire said later, *'I thought he was very funny.'*

(2006)

On the same day he popped into the library at Thomas Bennett Community College in Crawley where children aged seven to 13 were studying and asked teacher Judith Jarvis:

'Can they all read?'

Flustered Judith replied: *'Yes they can, Your Majesty,'* as the Duke wandered off roaring with laughter.

(2006)

An official at a Canadian airport asked the Duke: *'What was your flight like Your Royal Highness?'*

Philip: *'Have you ever flown in a plane?'*

Official: *'Oh yes, Sir, many times.'*

Philip: *'Well, it was just like that.'*

Prime Minister David Cameron identified this as his favourite Philip comment when he paid tribute to him in the House of Commons on his 90th birthday in 2011.

On a visit to open the new headquarters of GB Airways at Gatwick Airport, Philip chatted to pilots and cabin crew and told them:

'When you think about all the publicity about planes being dangerous to fly in, I wonder, why aren't all of you dead?'

(2000)

On arriving at GB's building he said:

'The first time I flew to Paris from Croydon Airport was in a four-seater bi-plane which travelled at 100 miles per hour and it was the size of a railway carriage. It was a great deal more comfortable than it is nowadays.'

(2000)

'I am sure many of you have noticed that there is no better way of finding out about a subject than having to speak about it.'

At a Buckingham Palace reception he was introduced to Oscar-winning actress Cate Blanchett.

Thinking she was a film technician he asked:

'Do you know how to fix my broken DVD player? There's a cord sticking out of the back and I don't know where it goes.'

(2008)

'I try to avoid laying inaugural stones because of their habit of getting lost, abandoned or stolen.'

(Early 1960s)

On a windy day in during celebrations for the Silver Jubilee, the Lord Mayor of London Sir Robin Gillett was leading the Queen and Philip up the steps of St Paul's Cathedral.

When a sudden gust of wind caught Sir Robin's ermine-trimmed robe, blowing it up like a balloon, Philip roared with laughter and said to the Queen:

'Look, I think the Lord Mayor is taking off!'

Sir Robin said later: *'I had a vision of flying up in the air like Mary Poppins leaving the Queen and Duke behind, but his little aside helped me over a very tense moment.'*

(1977)

At a Buckingham Palace dinner for his Duke of Edinburgh Award World Fellowship, Philip listened spellbound to tenor Russell Watson, who gave a stirring rendition of Jerusalem.

As he ended he said:

'That was magnificent, but why do you need a bloody microphone? They could have heard you in outer space.'

He then turned to the singer's partner Louise Harris and added:

'You must go deaf listening to him all the time.'

Russell said: *'I took it all as the greatest possible compliment.'*

(2011)

After the 2003 Royal Variety Show he met musician and TV presenter Myleene Klass in the line-up and told her:

'You're fit aren't you!'

(2003)

On a tour of East London he watched a fashion show with the Queen and then told model Somonah Achadoo:

'Your hair is too long. You should get it cut for the fifties.'

(2002)

To Welsh singer Katherine Jenkins:

'How are your vocal chords?'

'Fine thank you.'

'No boils or warts on them yet?'

(2006)

On a state visit to Slovenia he told tourism professor Dr Maja Uran:

'Tourism is just national prostitution. Tourists ruin cities.'

(2008)

On a visit to Canada the Mayor of Calgary gave Philip a Stetson hat.

'Not another one!' groaned the Prince, adding, *'Oh well, I suppose I can use it for a pot and put some flowers in it!'*

The Mayor got revenge later on the same visit when he then presented Philip with a spread of antlers. He told the Prince:

'Don't ask me what to do with them, and I won't tell you where to stick them!'

(1969)

Visiting the Chelsea Flower Show the Prince met Jamie Duries, designer of the Australian garden.

Philip said: *'I like your tree fern.'*

To which Jamie replied: *'It's not a tree fern, it's a member of the cycad family, it's a* macrozamia moore.'

Philip turned away muttering, *'I didn't want a bloody lecture!'*

(2008)

Talking about Universities:

'The first five hundred years of any institution are always the most difficult.'

In the early 1970s Philip was holidaying with his family at a remote cottage near the Inverpolly Nature Reserve 80 miles from Inverness.

He was driving on a lonely road with local naturalist Rob Tweddle when they came across a green Morris Minor stuck in a ditch.

Two astonished female teachers looked on as Philip and Rob lifted the car back onto the road.

Rob, now in his eighties, revealed in a 2011 article that the Prince told them:

'Now don't do that again,' before they drove off, leaving the women open-mouthed.

During a visit to Warburton's bakery in Bolton, the Prince met local council official Sean Harriss.

'Are you the Town Clerk,' asked Philip.

'No, I'm the chief executive.'

'That's a ridiculous title,' said the Duke, adding, *'Where's your wig?'*

(2009)

To Councillors on Ryde, Isle of Wight, who were wearing their ceremonial robes during a visit:

'You look like you are wearing dressing gowns!'

(1965)

The Queen and the Duke were visiting St Mary's on the Scilly Isles when Philip approached Sue and Clive Kirby from Bedfordshire. When told they were moving to the Islands the following month, he asked:

'Why? Do you like fish?'

A bemused Sue said: *'It was a strange remark.'*

(2011)

At a tree-planting ceremony in Hyde Park, the Queen met 16 year-old Army cadet Stephen Menary, who lost an arm and most of his sight in an IRA bomb attack.

When the Queen asked him how much he could see, Philip interjected:

'Not a lot, judging by the tie he's wearing.'

(2002)

As the Bishop of Norwich arrived at Sandringham to be guest preacher, Philip asked him:

'Are you happy clappy?'

To which the Bishop replied: *'No I'm smells and bells!'*

The Archbishop of York told this story in the House of Lords in 2011 while paying tribute to Philip on his 90th birthday.

In 1979, the Queen and Philip were guests at a reception in the White House hosted by President Jimmy Carter.

Butler Lynwood Westray approached the Prince and asked him:

'Your Majesty, [he should have called him Your Royal Highness] would you like a cordial?'

Philip replied: 'I'll take one if you let me serve you.'

He then spent the next fifteen minutes having a drink and a chat with astonished Lynwood and another butler.

(1979)

The Duke was standing beside David Sheppard, the Bishop of Liverpool, on board the Royal Yacht Britannia at Pier Head in the City when the brass band struck up with the hymn *The Lord is my shepherd.*

Philip whispered out of the corner of his mouth:

'Bishop, they're playing your tune!'

(1977)

At a reception in Liverpool following the Maundy money service the Queen and Philip were heading back to the Royal Train for the trip to London.

The Prince helped himself to a couple of extra cans of brown ale and put them into his jacket saying:

'It's for the onward journey!'

(2004)

On a visit to the Police Retraining Centre in County Down, Northern Ireland, Philip almost tripped on some steps and then spotted a shirtless man receiving physiotherapy.

'All that pushing and pulling, bloody agony,' he said, adding, *'It's hard to say whether physios actually do anything.'*

(2009)

To the Mayor of Slough David Macisaac when he was first appointed:

'Are you going to put on weight with all the meals you attend as Mayor?'

A few months later at a reception he patted him on the stomach and said:

'I told you you would get fat!'

Said David, *'He is an amazing man and I hope he never changes.'*

In San Francisco he met Mayor Dianne Feinstein and five female officials before remarking:

'Aren't there any male officials? This is a nanny city!'

(1983)

'To understand what ministers (politicians) are sometimes saying you must buy a gobbledegook dictionary and add an arbitrary ten years to every promise they make.'

(1960)

On Britain's manufacturing problems he told Panorama:

'Our rate of increase in productivity is lower than most countries in Europe – that may have something to do with the fact that we haven't got enough people technically trained in industry.

'We know perfectly well that people in this country have got a remarkable talent for things if they know how to do them.'

(1961)

On a visit to Sheffield's Hallam University he was shown a plastic dummy which talked, used in medical training.

As the dummy lay in bed saying: *'I don't feel well,'* Philip laughed and replied:

'Frankly you don't look well!'

(2008)

Meeting Duke of Edinburgh Award Scheme participants at a St James's Palace reception, one told him he had been doing conservation work in the jungle of Belize, Central America, where the SAS trained.

'It's a lovely part of the world, a bit like Sussex in places,' joked the Duke.

(2008)

Visiting a high rise block of flats he told one resident:

'The best thing that ever happened was when they were knocked down.

'They were a disaster most of them. They're all right for elderly people but not for families.'

(2008)

To a young man who told him he had been working with the Samaritans:

'Ah, the Samaritans, you didn't try to commit suicide did you?'

(2011)

At a lunch for AbFab, part of the Federation of London Youth Clubs, he said:

'Babies are born totally ignorant and totally inexperienced and they've all got to grow up and acquire experience and understanding.

'If you don't give young people the opportunities to find out about life, to find out what is worth doing and to be able to develop their capacity and their physical abilities, then they are never going to get anywhere.'

(2008)

'You find that lunches are seldom free.'

(2008)

'All original thinkers have a quality you can recognise.

'All architects wear ties with horizontal stripes, for instance, or no ties at all.'

(2009)

After the AGM of the National Playing Fields Association, Philip introduced fund-raiser Gyles Brandreth to a distinguished looking Asian man and said:

'This is the President of Pakistan.'

Brandreth was struggling to find small talk when Philip returned, saying:

'How are you two getting on?'

Realising Brandreth was out of his depth he said:

'He's the President of the Pakistan Playing Fields Association you idiot.

'He's not General Zia. Does he look like General Zia? Good God man, do you know anything?'

(1984)

Singer Alesha Dixon met Philip in the artists line-up after the Queen's Jubilee concert at Buckingham Palace.

She had appeared on stage with the group Mis-Teeq in a revealing costume.

'Aren't you cold dear?' asked Philip.

She replied: *'What are you going to do, lend me your jacket then?'*

(2002)

'Poverty is no longer absolute, it is relative.'

'Subsidised housing has greatly reduced homelessness.'

(1994)

As he sat with the Queen in the royal box at the Royal Variety Show watching a male stripping scene from *The Full Monty*, Philip told biographer Gyles Brandreth:

'Don't worry, she's been to Papua New Guinea and seen it all before!'

(2001)

At a Buckingham Palace lunch royal biographer Lady Antonia Fraser finds herself alone with Philip:

'What are you writing at the moment?'

'The Six Wives of Henry VIII.'

'Why do people always say Henry VIII and his six wives as if it was all one word? There is plenty more to say about Henry.'

'Oh yes, Sir, there is. He was a wonderful musician.'

Philip: *'He was a wonderful military strategist, a fighter, he bashed the French. HE BASHED THE FRENCH!'*

(1990)

Presented with a pair of green Bermuda shorts on a visit to the island he said:

'I'm not going to put them on now.'

(2009)

It doesn't look like much work goes on at this University.'

Overheard at Bristol University's engineering facility, which had been closed so that he could officially open it.

(2005)

On a visit to Hull he arrived at a women's centre and enquired:

'Still downtrodden then?'

Later he met victims of bad floods, many of who had lost their homes. Bidding farewell to Council leader Carl Minns, he said: *'Keep your head above water!'*

(2009)

After the Royal Variety performance the Queen and Philip met the cast backstage. *Britain's Got Talent* judges Simon Cowell and Piers Morgan had appeared to introduce singer Paul Potts.

When he came to them Philip asked:

'You're judges, is that right?'

'Yes, Sir,' replied Morgan.

'So,' said the Prince, looking back at Cowell before pointing to Paul Potts, *'you sponge off him then?'*

(2007)

'The man who invented the red carpet needed his head examined.'

To his Brazilian hosts who made every effort to greet him in style.

(1968)

At a Buckingham Palace garden party he met a woman who said she was expecting her second child.

'I hope you can afford your hat,' he told her.

(2012)

At a formal reception for peers and MPs in Parliament he met Tory MP Therese Coffey who said: *'Isn't it a lovely day, Sir?'*

He grunted, *'So far.'*

(2012)

To President Barack Obama at Buckingham Palace who told him he'd just met the leaders of the UK, China and Russia:

'Can you tell the difference between them?'

(2009)

'That's a nice tie ... do you have any knickers in that material?'

Discussing the tartan design for the Papal visit with then Scottish Tory leader Annabel Goldie.

(2010)

On over long church sermons:

'The mind cannot absorb what the backside cannot endure.'

'All money nowadays seems to be produced with a natural homing instinct for the treasury.'

Bemoaning the rate of British tax.

(1963)

Canadian quartet The Tenors impressed the Queen at a Diamond Jubilee performance at Windsor Castle – beforehand Philip had told them:

'I hope your voices don't break in the show.'

(2012)

To a woman solicitor:

'I thought it was against the law these days for a woman to solicit.'

(1987)

At a Buckingham Palace reception a guest said to the Queen:

'Thank you for having us Ma'am.'

Philip asked: *'What did he say?'*

The Queen replied: *'Thank you for having us.'*

The Prince said: *'Ah Harrogate, nice place.'*

(2001)

Philip accompanied the Queen when she visited Peterborough Cathedral to distribute the Royal Maundy money, then a service usually performed in London. After the service they went on a walkabout through the city. Philip, displaying his knowledge of the city's history, but oblivious of the fact that large sections of its inhabitants were not so well informed, was heard to quip to a bystander:

'I suppose you're an old soke!'

Speaking on birth control and a suggestion to limit the number of children per family:

'You can't expect to go on a bender and not expect a hangover.'

(1968)

On a visit to NASA HQ in Houston, Texas, he was put in the command seat of a simulated space capsule, which he had to dock by himself.

Asked what it was like he replied:

'It was like a bloody great mechanical copulator.'

(1991)

On a trip to Malta he asked an engaged couple in their 30s:

'How long have you two been at it?'

(2007)

Talking about Windsor Castle:

'An American tourist asked why they built the castle so close to Heathrow airport.'

Angry about modern day televisions:

'To work out how to operate a TV set you practically have to make love to the thing. You have to lie on the floor with a torch and magnifying glass. They put the controls on the bottom so you have to lie on the floor, and then if you want to record something the recorder is underneath, so you end up lying on the floor with a torch in your teeth, a magnifying glass and an instruction book. Either that or you have to employ a grandson of age ten to do it for you.

'And why can't you have a handset that people who are not ten years old can actually read?'

(2009)

Talking to MPs about the use of multi-coloured condoms by Thais:

'They choose yellow if they are happy and black if they are in mourning.'

Speaking about the Apollo space programme:

*'It seems to me that it's the best way of wasting money that I know of.
I don't think investments on the Moon pay a very high dividend.'*

(1968)

In Ghana he asked an MP:

'How many members of Parliament do you have?'

When told 200, he replied:

*'That's about the right number. We have 650 and most of them are a
complete bloody waste of time.'*

(1999)

On the same visit to Ghana he was shown a strip of brass laid in
a churchyard that marked the line of the Greenwich Meridian.

He told British Deputy High Commissioner Craig Murray:

'A line in the ground, eh? Very nice!'

(1999)

On the Queen's historic visit to Ireland they toured the
Guinness Storehouse in Dublin and were presented with a pint
of the black stuff.

'Is it made with Liffey water?' asked Philip.

(2011)

On a visit to the Samuel Whitbread Community College in Clifton, Bedfordshire, the Duke popped his head round the door of teacher Wendy Hill's science class and asked:

'Is there any sign of intelligent life in this classroom?'

Flustered, she replied: *'I wouldn't know.'* To which Philip retorted:

'Well you should know!'

Later Wendy said: *'I consider it a privilege to have been so soundly ticked off by Prince Philip – it made my day.'*

At a Palace reception honouring Australians, Philip met Joe Kerr, husband of Gill Hicks, who lost both legs in the July 2005 London bombings.

'You're not Australian!' said Philip.

'No, actually I'm not important, I'm just here because of my wife,' said Joe.

'Tell me about it!' said the Prince, walking off chuckling to himself.

(2006)

The Queen and Philip visited the HQ of the Canadian Broadcasting Corporation in Toronto when he approached two young women workers and asked them:

'Shouldn't you be at home watching your own programmes?'

(2002)

At a Holyroodhouse garden party an elderly couple sheltered under a golf umbrella with 'Renault' written on it. At the time a TV advert for Renault featured a couple shaking their bottoms.

Philip approached the pair, wiggled his behind and said:

'Do you do this?'

(2006)

On a visit to Oxford University Philip entered student Faizal Patel's room and spotted a traditional Egyptian Shisha pipe.

Thinking it was for smoking pot, Philip asked him:

'Are you involved in that sort of activity?'

He then asked the college master: *'You let students do this?'*

(2005)

Meeting chef Heston Blumenthal from the Fat Duck in Bray:

'I gather we are close neighbours.'

The following year he took his staff to the world famous restaurant for a Christmas celebration.

(2008)

Chairing a lecture at the Royal Society of Arts, a woman asked him about delays to the Athens Olympics.

'It's Paris that has the problems, look at Charles de Gaulle airport,' replied the Duke.

(2004)

On a visit to the new GCHQ building in Cheltenham, Labour MP Chris Mullin asked Philip about the ultra-modern design, saying: *'Would Charles approve?'*

'Charles who?' replied the Duke.

(2004)

Ruthless Mexican President Gustavo Diaz Ordaz crushed a protest before the 1968 Olympics which resulted in several hundred deaths.

In a letter sent to Harold Macmillan shortly after he had met him in 1964, Philip wrote: *'I had a most interesting conversation with President Ordaz. I found him an easy and interesting conversationalist with a pleasant sense of humour. He liked gardening.'*

(Letter released by the Public Record Office in 2003)

Talking about modern day manners:

'I think there are some things which are rather disappointing. This general rather bitter, sour attitude that so many people have to life at the moment. This aggression, boorishness and rudery – you do owe a certain amount of politeness to each other.'

(2000)

The Queen and Philip were at the Association of Chartered Certified Accountants dinner when the Duke livened up proceedings with this joke:

'Three accountants go for a job interview and are asked to add up two plus two.

'The first accountant thinks for a bit and says, "Five".

'The second punches the numbers into his calculator and comes up with "Four".

'While the third replies, "The answer can be whatever you want".'

(2004)

---

d:

...al!'

(2008)

...le that will produce more ... an udder attached to it. They ...sty of an animal. There must be

...ct that milk is actually cheaper than ...bizarre to me.'

(2009)

...m not a bunny-hugger, one who simply loves animals. ...re concerned about how you treat a donkey in Sicily than ...on.'

(2011)

*'Everybody has to have a sense of duty. A duty to society, to their fam[...]
I mean, you name it. If you haven't got a sense of duty you get the [...]
of community we have now. Look around. Mugging and drug[...]
abuse – intellectual abuse, intellectual mugging.'*

'Anyone concerned about their dignity would be well advised to keep away from horses.'

After a meal of venison at Magdalen College, Oxford, Philip spotted a herd of deer in the grounds and asked the bursar:

'How many of those buggers did you have to shoot for lunch then?'

On being told the supply had come from Kent then:

'Well, don't tell Charles because he likes everyone to buy lo[...]

On farming economics and regulations:

*'They are constantly trying to produce cat[...]
milk and less cow – like a hat-rack with[...]
can't really go on making such a tra[...]
a limit to this.*

*'Even more ridiculous is the f[...]
bottled water. It seems quite[...]*

*'I'm not green. [...]
People are m[...]
conservati[...]*

Asked by a farm magazine if conservation was too important to be left to conservationists, he replied:

'I would say that farming is too important to be left to farmers.'

'We've got extraordinary diversity on this globe and it seems awfully silly for us to destroy it.'

(2011)

On a visit to the Shakespeare theatre in Stratford-Upon-Avon he was told by actor Geoffrey Freshwater that he had to skin a real dead rabbit on stage as part of his role as Corin in *As You Like It*.

'There will be a lot of blood – what do you do with it all?' asked Philip.

(2011)

On shooting and the management of birds, such as crows and magpies which prey on game birds and threaten the songbird populations:

'If you are interested in species you want to see these birds around, but you don't want to have so many of them that they interfere with another population that you want to see and exploit.

'So I see the point of protecting these birds, but I don't see that blanket protection is the best way of doing it.'

(Interview with the *Shooting Times* 2009)

Making a case for there being no moral difference between killing animals for sport or money he angered women's groups saying:

'I don't think a prostitute is more moral than a wife, but they are doing the same thing. It is really rather like saying it is perfectly all right to commit adultery providing you don't enjoy it.'

(1988)

On organic farming:

'Organic farming is not an absolute certainty that it's quite as useful as it sounds. You've got to be emotionally committed to it – but if you stand back and be open minded about it, it is quite difficult to really find where it has been a real benefit.'

(2008)

On shooting at Sandringham:

'I think that shooting is effectively cropping, and what you do is take the surplus and make sure that you have a crop next year.'

(2009)

When an animal rights demonstrator kept shouting slogans through a megaphone at Cambridge University Philip turned to her and said sarcastically:

'Can't you think of anything else to say?'

(2003)

'Come on you bloody idiots!'

Said to his horses during driving trials in Cumbria.

(2004)

On a tour of South Africa in the 1990s, Philip was at a reception when the subject of pandas and their reluctance to breed came up. One guest argued that the bears became too attached to their zoo keepers in captivity.

'Well, then, the logical solution would seem to be dress one of the pandas up as a zoo-keeper so that the other one fancies it,' the Prince argued.

'Ninety-five per cent of the whole of the Atlantic rain forest in Brazil has disappeared in the last hundred years. There is simply nowhere for the animals to live.'

'At the basis of it all is this colossal increase in the human population.'

'It [man] is one of the living species of the planet but it is reaching plague proportions.'

(1984)

To the Edinburgh University Union about the environment:

'We know enough to appreciate what is happening and the need to take care.

'Pollution is no longer a matter of local incidents, today it has the whole biosphere in its grip.'

'Still largely unnoticed and unrecognised, the process of destroying our natural environment is gathering speed and momentum. If we fail to cope with this challenge, all the other problems will pale into insignificance.'

(1969)

Speaking to the World Wildlife Fund congress in London:

'It is an old cliché to say that the future is in the hands of the young. This is no longer true.

'The quality of life to be enjoyed or the existence to be survived by our children and future generations is in our hands now.'

(1970)

Talking about churches and faiths getting involved in protecting the environment:

'It seemed to me that most religions attributed the world to some special creation and I said look, if you believe that God created the world then you ought to take an interest in its well-being.'

(2008)

'Partridges are incredibly stupid birds.'

(2008)

'Conservation is not a romantic business. It is a very practical business as you are trying to ensure that as many different species of wildlife can co-exist.'

'It is making choices. For example you'd get practically no wild pheasants if you didn't control the foxes.'

'You wouldn't get any partridges if you didn't control the rats.'

(2008)

'People don't like to admit it but cats catch an enormous number of small wild birds. But people are very attached to their cats – it's a fact of life.'

(2008)

'The food prices are going up – everyone thinks it's to do with not enough food, but it's really that demand is too great, too many people.'

'It's embarrassing and no-one knows how to handle it, because nobody wants their family life to be interfered with by the Government.'

(2008)

'People go on about this carbon footprint, but they fail to realise that the amount of carbon going into the atmosphere is entirely dependent on the number of people living on the Earth.'

'There are now 60 million people in this country. This country had three million people in Elizabeth I's day.'

(2009)

'Culling is vital. How are the poor countries going to pay for (their wildlife) unless they can get an economic benefit from it?'

(1992)

Asked to write a prayer about the environment for a children's charity book, the Prince showed his softer side:

'O Lord, the creator of the Universe and author of the laws of nature, inspire in us thy servants the will to ensure the survival of all the species

of animals and plants, which you have given to share this planet with us.

'Help us to understand that we have a responsibility for them and that 'having dominion' does not mean that you have given us the right to exploit the living world without thought for the consequences.

'Through him who taught us that Solomon in all his glory could not compare with the beauty of the flowers of the field.'

(1998)

THE COMMANDER:
Splice the Mainbrace!

Prince Philip had a distinguished career in the Royal Navy and was heading for the top when George VI died in 1952.

Princess Elizabeth became Queen on the death of her father and Philip decided his number one priority was to support his wife.

But there was a hint of regret in a 2011 BBC interview with Fiona Bruce when he said it might have helped the Queen to have someone by her side who was 'professionally qualified in something and not just traipsing around.'

Philip joined the battleship HMS *Ramillies* in 1940 as an 18 year-old Midshipman. In 1941 he was appointed to HMS *Valiant* in the Mediterranean Fleet, based in Alexandria.

He was Mentioned in Despatches for operating searchlights during the Battle of Matapan against the Italian navy.

While serving on the Destroyer Escort HMS *Wallace* he was promoted to Lieutenant and soon after, aged 21, First Lieutenant and second in command.

In 1944 he was made First Lieutenant of the Fleet Destroyer HMS *Whelp*, which was sent to the Far East.

In 1950 he was promoted to Lieutenant Commander and was stationed in Malta, where his wife (they married in 1947) was able to join him.

In 1952, by now a Commander, he had to break the news to Elizabeth that her father had died while they were in Kenya en route to Australia.

In January 1953, after 14 years service, the Duke gave up his active career in the Navy.

He was promoted to Admiral of the Fleet, and appointed Field Marshal and Marshal of the Royal Air Force.

In 2011, to mark his 90th birthday, the Queen gave Philip the ancient title of Lord High Admiral, a post she had held since 1964.

'Watching a parade through a bearskin is like watching it through a thunderstorm.'

While serving on HMS *Valiant* the ship helped to sink two Italian cruisers within five minutes.

Philip said later, *'It was as near murder as anything could be in wartime. The cruisers just burst into tremendous sheets of flame.'*

On a visit to the D-Day museum in Portsmouth, Philip asked 55 year-old Linda Rivers:

'Where is your Land Army badge?'

She was born nine years after World War Two ended.

(2009)

To a soldier whose head was injured by shrapnel from an explosive device packed with ball-bearings:

'Does your head rattle?'

(2008)

Philip was in the mess at RAF HQ in Bahrain when a waiter served him a gin and tonic. When he asked for 1 shilling and sixpence, Philip laughed and said:

'Sorry old man, but sadly I do not carry money.'

Another officer settled the bill.

(1969)

On a lengthy tour of the Royal Navy's HMS *Boxer* he got bored and exclaimed:

*'Not another f****ing chamber!'*

(2008)

Visiting the Defence Academy in Shrivenham, Wiltshire, he was shown a hand grenade with a mini parachute attached.

'I thought Heath Robinson was dead,' said Philip.

On the same visit, as he was about to pull the curtain on a plaque recording his visit, he remarked:

'You are about to see the world's most expert plaque unveiler at work.'

(2011)

On being forced to wait at Newcastle airport, dressed in full Field Marshal uniform, Philip paced up and down the tarmac muttering:

'Where's my bloody aeroplane?'

Old soldier Tom Gilhooley was standing on parade in the hot sun beside the Normandy beaches at the 60th anniversary of the D-day landings.

'You're going to pay for it standing in this hot sun,' the Duke told him.

An hour later Philip returned and saw Tom, his face glowing red.

'I told you you'd pay for it,' he laughed.

(2004)

On a visit to a Territorial Army barracks in Canterbury, Kent, he asked veteran TA soldier Frank Smith:

'What do you do in civilian life?'

He replied: *'I'm a refuse collector.'*

'What you take people in and give them shelter?' said the Prince,

'No, I chuck black sacks into a dustcart.'

Philip turned to some officers and said: *'Oh, I see. For God's sake laugh then!'*

(1984)

Explaining his piercing whistle as he called for an encore to a singer at a dinner party:

'I learned it the hard way – getting taxis in the London blackout.'

On a visit to RAF Kinloss a woman told him she was going to become a dental nurse.

'It'll be like pulling teeth,' exclaimed Philip.

(2011)

Presenting prizes to cadets on HMS *Devonshire*:

'I am afraid that I am in no position to offer you any advice about your future in the Navy as I only served about half a Dog Watch myself.'

(1953)

Although an excellent pilot, some tried to discourage him from moving onto fast Meteors. When it was pointed out that few RAF Air Marshals had flown solo in jets he replied:

'But I am the RAF's youngest Air Marshal.'

Speak‎ ⋯ ⋯bers of the Burma Star Association:

'I ⋯ ⋯ but

⋯ the most

⋯ disappointing. I

⋯ promoted to commander and the fact was just starting

⋯ interesting part of my naval career was just starting

But my first duty was to serve the Queen in the best way I

When asked at a dinner on the eve of Trooping the Colour if he would be riding the following day, the 85 year-old Prince replied to Lord Guthrie, former Chief of the Defence Staff:

'No, I'm not – the horse is too old!'

(2006)

After a dinner at the Headquarters Mess of the Royal Artillery, Woolwich:

'I am afraid I don't know much about Gunners and so before coming to Woolwich I tried to find out something. I asked the nearest soldier, but if I repeated what he said I fear I would not be asked to the mess again.'

(1952)

Asked how he felt about giving up his naval career:

'Well, I mean, how long is a piece of string?

'I don't know how difficul

had just been

inte

'Any bloody fool can lay a wreath at the thingamy.'

Interviewed by Jeremy Paxman for his book *On Royalty*.

(2006)

On the Royal Yacht *Britannia*, which was decommissioned in 1997:

'She should have had her steam turbines taken out and diesel engines put in.'

'She was sound as a bell, and she could have gone on for another 50 years.'

(2011)

On a visit to the Air Training Corps in King's Lynn, Norfolk, he was shown some short wave radios.

'Can you listen to anything interesting on them? It doesn't get into the police network?'

He then met a cadet who had been gliding.

'Have you been taken up and made to feel sick yet?'

(2008)

MEDIA MONKEYS

Philip has always been highly critical of the press, blaming the media for nearly destroying his family over the years with negative reporting.

But he was the first member of the monarchy to make TV programmes himself, and famously it was his idea to allow the cameras in to film the Queen and her children for the fly-on-the-wall documentary *Royal Family* in 1969.

The programme was a sensation, watched by three-quarters of the British population. But critics said it destroyed the mystique of royalty, and the Queen regretted taking part.

It has not been shown in full for 40 years, but Philip has always been a moderniser, and he could see the monarchy needed to be brought into the TV age.

Although he rails at reporters and fumes at photographers, the Prince has a collection of cuttings and cartoons in which he features.

'I don't grill newsmen for breakfast.'

(1965)

At a polo match in Jamaica in the 1960s he told photographers:

'You bloody load of clots – you could take pictures like this any Sunday at home at Windsor.'

To TV reporters with a long microphone on a pole:

'Here comes that bloody machine again – why don't you stick it up your ...'

At a reception in Trinidad in the 1960s he once turned to reporters and told them:

'You have ruined my life.'

Reporter John Shaw was covering an after lunch meeting between the Duke and the Small Business Association.

'Who the hell are you?' he asked the newsman as he took notes.

'I'm John Shaw of the Press Association.'

Philip: *'What the hell are you doing here? No one told me the press was going to be here. This is disgraceful, I'm off!'*

(1969)

To the matron of a Caribbean hospital:

'You have mosquitoes – I have the press.'

(1966)

A Scottish photographer was told by his picture desk to take a shot of Philip arriving at Aberdeen airport. He was then told to snap him when he left.

'Has my face changed that much in 12 hours?' asked Philip.

The photographer, who had been waiting around for hours in the cold, said: *'F*** you!'*

Philip laughed it off and went over to commiserate.

(1970)

'Damn fool question!'

To BBC reporter Caroline Wyatt at an Elysee Palace banquet when asked if the Queen was enjoying her stay.

(2006)

'I reckon I have done something right if I don't appear in the media. So I've retreated – quite consciously – so as not to be an embarrassment.'

(2006)

On Rupert Murdoch and his newspapers:

'His anti-establishment views really pulled the plug on an awful lot of things that we hold to be quite reasonable and sensible institutions.'

(2006)

Asked when press coverage took a turn for the worse:

'After Rupert Murdoch bought the Today *newspaper from Eddie Shah.*

'Day after day there was a derogatory story about one member of the family or another.'

On a visit to Gibraltar he was feeding the famous Barbary Apes when he quipped:

'Which are the apes and which are the reporters?'

He once saw a Pakistani photographer fall out of a tree and remarked:

'I hope to God he breaks his bloody neck!'

In 2011 Author Tim Heald revealed how every day, wherever he is, Philip makes 'a grab' for the newspapers saying:

'Let's see what I'm supposed to have done wrong yesterday.'

Talking about allegations he has had affairs he once told his cousin Patricia Mountbatten:

'When I see the tabloids I think I might as well have done it!'

As ITN reporter Romilly Weeks was presenting a live piece to camera in Malta about the Queen and Philip's visit, the Duke crept up behind her and tried to put her off.

He waited until the end and asked: *'Finished?'*

Romilly burst into fits of laughter.

(2007)

The Sun's royal photographer Arthur Edwards was sitting in his car outside the stables at Sandringham. Suddenly Philip popped up and said to him:

'Having a good snoop are we?'

(1980)

In the 1980s a group of tabloid reporters were gathered at the gates of Sandringham Palace in Norfolk when Philip roared up in his Land Rover.

'You people are scum!' he bawled.

One royal correspondent bravely retorted: *'We may be scum sir, but we are the crème de la scum.'*

To a French photographer:

'Vous êtes fou, restez chez vous.' (You are a fool, go home.)

'I didn't want to do this interview.'

To Fiona Bruce for the BBC programme *The Duke at 90*.

(2011)

'I don't see why people shouldn't know what's going on. Much better that they should know than speculate.'

(2011)

'The media is a professional intruder – you can't complain about it.'

(2011)

Asked if he thought the press had been unfair to him he replied:

'Yes, occasionally. But they have their own agenda and you just have to live with that.'

(2011)

'Yes, I made a conscious decision to talk to the media – but not about me, only about what I'm doing, what I'm supporting.'

(1999)

During the furore over the 'slitty-eyed' remark, an American female reporter was seen by Philip pulling her eyes into slits as she joked with colleagues.

'What's the matter with you?' he asked. *'Too much sun?'*

(1986)

His most famous gaffe came in 1986 when he told a British student in China:

'If you stay here much longer you'll be slitty-eyed.'

Asked about the remark he said:

'I'd forgotten about it. But for one particular reporter, Mr Hamilton from The Times, who overheard it, it wouldn't have come out.

'What's more the Chinese weren't worried about it, so why should anyone else?'

(2011)

Just before filming in a car at Sandringham for a 2008 documentary called *The Duke*, interviewer Sir Trevor McDonald wanted to do a sound check and asked Philip:

'Can we ask you to count to five?'

The Prince replied: *'What about you counting to five?'*

When McDonald did so, Philip carried on:

'Six seven eight nine ten!'

(2008)

'Given the way of the British press, I wouldn't have got far in the Navy. Every promotion would have been seen as me being treated as a special case.'

(1999)

'I go out of my way to line people up for the photographers, to make sure everyone in the group is in the picture, to make sure the photographers have got the shot they need.

'Of course, they always want one more – they're never satisfied.'

(1999)

'The press have turned us into a soap opera.'

(1999)

'When we were in South Africa some years ago, I flew up to Kimberley and was persuaded to take some media people with me.

'On the way back, one of them said to my policeman that it had been a complete waste of time as I had not put my foot in it.'

(1999)

Female reporter: 'I wondered if you might like to talk to me?'

'Well, you can carry on wondering.'

(2005)

On a visit to the new British Embassy in Berlin:

Journalist: *'Your Royal Highness, could you give us your view on the building?'*

Philip: *'No.'*

(2000)

'I have frequently been misrepresented. I don't hate the press. I find a lot of it is very unpalatable. But if that's the way they want to behave well....'

(1992)

To journalists and photographers getting too close:

'Don't jostle the Queen!'

'You cannot take quotations in newspapers seriously. It so happens that it is perfectly legal to put anything in a newspaper in quotation marks, and there is nothing you can do about it. You have no copyright on what other people say you said.

'There's no point in talking about it.'

(1992)

For years there were rumours Philip had an affair with singer Pat Kirkwood.

In 1988 he wrote to her from Balmoral:

'I am very sorry indeed to hear that you have been pestered about that ridiculous "rumour".

'The trouble is that certain things seem to get into journalist ' folklore' and it is virtually impossible to get it out of the system.

'Much as I would like to put a stop to this, and many other similar stories about other members of the family, we have found that, short of starting libel proceedings, there is absolutely nothing to be done.

'Invasion of privacy, invention and false quotations are the bane of our existence.'

(1988)

...mes.

...pic Games
...erybody there

...!'

(1952)

...the game in history.

...ed in a game during a recruiting
...th a torn shirt and all the players

...red by his father not to play anymore,
...ill or more probably because every time he
...wondered why he had a black eye.'

(1957)

The next year from Sandringham he wrote to deplore th[e...]
that Kirkwood and her husband had been besieged by [...]

'I am deeply sorry that you have had this very unpleas[...]
with the press.

'After nearly 40 years of such treatment, I am mor[...]
this sort of thing, so please do not feel any anxiet[...]
can only hope that the matter will now be dr[...]

'There must be a limit to the amount of '[...]
a stone.

'Philip.'

To an Olympic Games audience in London, 1948:   (1948)

'I wish to contradict a rumour.

'You will NOT see a familiar figure bearing the Olympic Torch on the opening day.'

At the Olympics in Helsinki :

'A lot of weird things have been written about the Olympic G[...]

'It's much more important to come away from the Oly[...]
with a good reputation and having made friends with e[...]
than to come back with a bagful of medals.

'On the other hand I have no objection to doing bot[...]

On football:

'Every now and then one gets glimpses o[...]

'Henry VIII is supposed to have joi[...]
march. He ultimately emerged w[...]
enlisted in the army.

'One of the James's was ord[...]
either because of the clothes [...]
appeared in public peopl[...]

Ruthless Mexican President Gustavo Diaz Ordaz crushed a protest before the 1968 Olympics which resulted in several hundred deaths.

In a letter sent to Harold Macmillan shortly after he had met him in 1964, Philip wrote: *'I had a most interesting conversation with President Ordaz. I found him an easy and interesting conversationalist with a pleasant sense of humour. He liked gardening.'*

(Letter released by the Public Record Office in 2003)

Talking about modern day manners:

'I think there are some things which are rather disappointing. This general rather bitter, sour attitude that so many people have to life at the moment. This aggression, boorishness and rudery – you do owe a certain amount of politeness to each other.'

(2000)

The Queen and Philip were at the Association of Chartered Certified Accountants dinner when the Duke livened up proceedings with this joke:

'Three accountants go for a job interview and are asked to add up two plus two.

'The first accountant thinks for a bit and says, "Five".

'The second punches the numbers into his calculator and comes up with "Four".

'While the third replies, "The answer can be whatever you want".'

(2004)

'Everybody has to have a sense of duty. A duty to society, to their family. I mean, you name it. If you haven't got a sense of duty you get the sort of community we have now. Look around. Mugging and drugs and abuse – intellectual abuse, intellectual mugging.'

(1992)

BLASTED BIRDS AND BLOODY BUNNY HUGGERS

The Prince has always had a keen interest in the environment and the conservation of nature, speaking out on such issues when they were far from fashionable.

He became the President of the British World Wildlife Fund in 1961, and the International President of the WWF in 1981, a post he held until 1996. He is now President Emeritus.

During his time many endangered species were saved, including the panda, the snow leopard, and the black rhino.

He is sometimes criticised for his hunting, shooting and fishing lifestyle, but he has never been on a foxhunt, and believes passionately that it is necessary to control the numbers of some animals on estates for the benefit of all.

For more than 40 years he has been warning of the dangers of over-population of the Earth by mankind, although of course he himself has four children!

'Anyone concerned about their dignity would be well advised to keep away from horses.'

After a meal of venison at Magdalen College, Oxford, Philip spotted a herd of deer in the grounds and asked the bursar:

'How many of those buggers did you have to shoot for lunch then?'

On being told the supply had come from Kent he quipped:

'Well, don't tell Charles because he likes everyone to buy local!'

(2008)

On farming economics and regulations:

'They are constantly trying to produce cattle that will produce more milk and less cow – like a hat-rack with an udder attached to it. They can't really go on making such a travesty of an animal. There must be a limit to this.

'Even more ridiculous is the fact that milk is actually cheaper than bottled water. It seems quite bizarre to me.'

(2009)

'I'm not green. I'm not a bunny-hugger, one who simply loves animals. People are more concerned about how you treat a donkey in Sicily than conservation.'

(2011)

For years there were rumours Philip had an affair with singer Pat Kirkwood.

In 1988 he wrote to her from Balmoral:

'I am very sorry indeed to hear that you have been pestered about that ridiculous "rumour".

'The trouble is that certain things seem to get into journalist 'folklore' and it is virtually impossible to get it out of the system.

'Much as I would like to put a stop to this, and many other similar stories about other members of the family, we have found that, short of starting libel proceedings, there is absolutely nothing to be done.

'Invasion of privacy, invention and false quotations are the bane of our existence.'

(1988)

The next year from Sandringham he wrote to deplore the news that Kirkwood and her husband had been besieged by newsmen.

'I am deeply sorry that you have had this very unpleasant experience with the press.

'After nearly 40 years of such treatment, I am more or less hardened to this sort of thing, so please do not feel any anxiety about my reaction – I can only hope that the matter will now be dropped.

'There must be a limit to the amount of blood you can squeeze out of a stone.

'Philip.'

(1989)

A SPORTING LIFE

Philip has always believed in the importance of keeping fit, and the role sport has to play in bringing people together.

At Gordonstoun he captained the school at cricket and hockey.

A keen sailor at numerous Cowes weeks, he became Admiral of the Royal Yacht Squadron and was President of the Royal Yachting Association.

For more than 20 years he played polo, retiring in 1971 with a handicap of 5. And from 1964 until 1986 he was President of the International Equestrian Federation.

He won one World Team Gold and three World and one European bronze medals after taking up competitive Carriage Driving. And when he gave up driving horses in 1986 he continued with a team of Fell ponies, taking part in the 2002 European Championships.

He was President of the Football Association from 1955 to 1958 and President of the MCC in 1950 and 1974.

Little wonder then that 'The Gaffer' has not been backward in coming forward with a few 'sporting gems.'

To an Olympic Games audience in London, 1948:

'I wish to contradict a rumour.

'You will NOT see a familiar figure bearing the Olympic Torch on the opening day.'

(1948)

At the Olympics in Helsinki :

'A lot of weird things have been written about the Olympic Games.

'It's much more important to come away from the Olympic Games with a good reputation and having made friends with everybody there than to come back with a bagful of medals.

'On the other hand I have no objection to doing both!'

(1952)

On football:

'Every now and then one gets glimpses of the game in history.

'Henry VIII is supposed to have joined in a game during a recruiting march. He ultimately emerged with a torn shirt and all the players enlisted in the army.

'One of the James's was ordered by his father not to play anymore, either because of the clothes bill or more probably because every time he appeared in public people wondered why he had a black eye.'

(1957)

In New York in 1957 the Queen and Prince Philip were given the traditional ticker tape welcome. As they were being ferried across the river they had a distant view of Brooklyn.

The Prince asked an official: *'That has a famous baseball team doesn't it?'*

'Yes, Sir,' said the official. *'We call them the.....'*

As he faltered, trying to remember the name, Philip came to the rescue: *'I know, you call them "dem bums".'*

(1957)

On American Football:

'We watched a game in America last week. I can't say it is a close relation to soccer but it's fascinating to watch and it's more like a campaign than anything else.'

(1957)

The Prince has some strong views on Olympic ceremonies.

Interviewed by the *Daily Telegraph*'s Sue Mott he said:

'Olympic opening and closing ceremonies ought to be banned.'

'Absolute bloody nuisances.'

'I have been to one that was absolutely, appallingly, awful.

'I was suddenly told – at Munich I think it was – that we couldn't have the main arena for show-jumping because it had to be prepared for the closing ceremony.

'What is the Olympics about, the competition or the closing ceremony? They're a pain in the neck.'

(2006)

On carriage driving:

'I took it up as a geriatric sport. I thought of it as a retirement exercise.

'I promise you when I set out I thought it would be a nice weekend activity, rather like a golfing weekend. Which it was, until some idiot asked me to be a member of the British team.'

(2006)

Asked during a Test Match Special how modern cricket could be improved:

'I only wish to God that some of their trousers fitted better!'

To a Chinese delegate worried about protocol at an Equestrian Federation meeting in Geneva:

'As far as we are concerned you can play Colonel Bogey and fly a pair of knickers from the flagpole as your team enters the arena.'

Asked if the carriage driving got in the way of his duties he replied:

'It's the other way round. The duties get in the way of the driving.'

(2006)

Asked by Sue Mott if carriage driving was risky for a man in his eighties he replied:

'You haven't got a bloody clue, have you?

'You've never seen anybody come to any harm, so why do you say it's dangerous? It's like climbing. People say, "Oh you can fall off." Well, they don't fall off. Not if they learn properly and if they're properly organised.'

(2006)

'It [carriage driving] is always great fun. When I started driving, I used to try to find people I could stay with so that I could drive. I now drive so that I can go and stay with people.'

(2004)

'Carriage driving is relatively friendly. Everybody knows each other.

'I was once criticised at a championship because I found the Hungarians walking around. They didn't have a car so I asked them to jump in.

'Someone said, "what are you doing, helping the enemy?" I said, "This is silly".'

(2004)

'I haven't got a message for anybody, thank you. I'm not trying to promote it like a soap powder. I mean, it's a sport for Christ's sake. If people want to take part, it's up to them.'

(2004)

'When did anybody take their eye out playing conkers?'

(2006)

To Sue Mott:

'What do you do for fun? Don't you actually DO anything, shove-ha'penny or something?'

(2006)

Asked if he had ever parachuted or bungee jumped he replied:

'No, I don't think I'd like my eyeballs to go out and then in again somehow.'

(2006)

'I am not really a talented spectator, frankly. Yes, it's quite fun to watch but it's not the be-all and end-all. I've had enough of it.'

'I did something like five Olympic Games as president of the FEI, when I was just standing around watching things. I'd rather do something.'

(2006)

On the day he had England test hero Tom Graveney caught off an off-break during a charity cricket match:

'He, of course, was then unmercifully teased by all his contemporaries. Every time I met him afterwards I always tactfully failed to mention it and he always brought it up.'

(2006)

'You've got to be a nut-case to go carriage driving – the best bit is when it's over.'

(2004)

After competing in Hungary he said:

'The most dangerous part of that tournament was visiting the Hungarian camp, because whatever the time of day, they gave you a glass of peach brandy and you were lucky to escape with your life.'

(2004)

On risk in sport:

'If you're climbing a mountain, there is a risk that your rope will break. So you get the best possible rope because you know the consequences.'

'What would really make it a risk is climbing up with a rotten rope – and then you're surprised when it breaks on you.'

(2004)

On sport in schools:

'Everything you do is based on competition unless some half-witted teacher seems to think it's bad for you.'

(2006)

Asked what he would do at the 2012 London Olympics, when he would be 91:

'As little as possible.'

(2006)

At a Buckingham Palace reception for British Paralympians Philip took one look at all the gold medals on display and said:

'There is so much gold in the room some should be donated to Gordon Brown to help ease the country's cash crisis.'

Medal winner Matt Shelham said: *'He was hilarious.'*

(2009)

When England's women cricketers visited Buckingham Palace to receive honours for beating Australia he told captain Clare Connor that her version of the Ashes trophy

'... looks like something cobbled together in a sixth-form woodwork class.'

(2006)

Speaking in the United States on the royal family's finances:

'We go into the red next year... I may have to give up polo.'

(1969)

Declining an offer to play polo during a visit to Pakistan, where the standard was high, he said:

'I went to Pakistan on serious business. If I'd gone there to play polo, I'd have got in some practice beforehand.'

After the Lowther Show driving trials were cancelled due to heavy rain, Philip was walking across muddy fields when he remarked:

'It's like walking on a fat lady's tummy.'

(2008)

As patron of the Lord's Taverners he wrote this preface to *The Boundary Book* by Leslie Frewin:

'I cannot claim to have an intimate knowledge of the Lord's Tavern but I do know that it has an atmosphere that cannot be ascribed to cricket alone!'

'Quite what it is that makes the Tavern such a very special place, I don't know. But there is something about this celebrated hostelry that can persuade an eminent Scottish playwright to stand and watch cricket in the company of perfectly strange Englishmen.'

'What is it that causes staid theatrical producers to finish rehearsals early on some trivial excuse, only to find themselves, ten minutes later, rubbing shoulders at the Tavern with their own actors who should be studying their lines?'

'And what prompts a renowned conductor to lay down his baton on a Saturday afternoon and look for a cab to St John's Wood? Just cricket?'

'Scientists one day may discover what controls the homing instinct of fish and birds but I hope they never try to analyse the urge of the Taverner to return to Lord's.'

(1962)

On a visit to the Lords Test Match he asked Australian head coach Tim Nielsen:

'Are you the team's scorer?'

(2009)

On the same day an MCC official asked him:

'Did you enjoy your lunch, Sir?'

Philip: *'Why do you ask that?'*

MCC man: *'I hoped the answer would be yes.'*

Philip: *'What a stupid question.'*

(2009)

While sailing at Cowes the crewman of a boat approaching Philip's yacht shouted out: 'Water!' – a term for moving out of the way – and then: 'Stavros!'

Philip shouted back:

'It's not Stavros and it's my wife's f***ing water so I'll do what I f***ing please!'

'I've been lucky and had very few things go wrong.'

'It's terrible for people who break things. Take Rooney. That must be really hideous for him at the high point of his career.'

(2006)

'Taking part in games and sports is very much part of the growing up process.

'Taking part in team games teaches you a respect for the law because you won't have a game unless you play according to the rules.

'The other thing you discover is that you cannot succeed entirely by yourself in a team game. You have to participate with the others.

'I think it also teaches that failure isn't the end of the world. You always bounce back again, and you may win next time.

'It is very important through life that you don't win all the time – occasionally you have to face a defeat.'

(2000)

On the Queen's historic visit to Ireland he met former Jordan team boss and BBC presenter Eddie Jordan and said:

'Ah! You're that funny chap who does the F1!'

(2011)

Sometimes, just occasionally, he is on the receiving end.

Before the 1968 Mexico Olympics Philip told the GB team that the lack of oxygen when competing so high above sea level was nothing to worry about, and he had played some very hard games of polo there.

At the end the boxer Chris Finnegan put his hand up.

'Yes, Mr Finnegan,' said the Prince.

Finnegan: *'Sir, you know when you said that you did not feel the effects when you played polo here?'*

'Yes, that is true.'

Finnegan: *'Well, did anyone think of asking the bleedin' horses?'*

(1968)

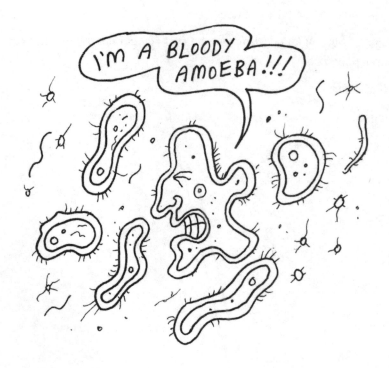

ON HIMSELF AND HIS FAMILY:
ROYAL REFLECTIONS

In 1997, at a lunch in London's Guildhall to mark their golden wedding, the Queen paid tribute to her husband, saying:

'He is someone who doesn't take easily to compliments. He has, quite simply, been my strength and stay all these years, and I, and his whole family, and this and many other countries, owe him a debt greater than he would ever claim or we shall ever know.'

No one could have put it better, as this amusing, reflective and sometimes poignant selection shows.

When Elizabeth became Queen in 1952 she was advised by Winston Churchill to call the Monarchy the House of Windsor. Philip complained to a friend:

'I am nothing but a bloody amoeba, the only man in the country not allowed to give his name to his own children.'

He was the first person to pay homage to the Queen at her Coronation in 1953. He knelt before her, held her hand and said:

'I, Philip Duke of Edinburgh, do become your liege man of life and limb; and of earthly worship; and faith and truth will I bear unto you,

to live and die, against all manner of folks.

'So help me God.'

(1953)

Asked about his childhood when his family fled from Greece and he was separated from his parents:

'I don't try to psychoanalyse myself.'

(2011)

Pressed in the same interview by Fiona Bruce for the BBC programme *The Duke at 90*, he was asked:

'Where was home?'

'Wherever I happened to be. It was no great deal. I just lived my life.'

Bruce: *But some people might...'*

'Well, some people might, I'm telling you what I felt.'

(2011)

Talking about his family escaping from Greece when he was a baby:

'They didn't have a cot – I was put in an orange box.'

(1998)

On the highly successful Duke of Edinburgh's Award Scheme:

'I've no reason to be proud.'

'It's satisfying that we've set up a formula that works but I don't run it. It's all fairly second-hand.'

'I didn't want my name attached to it. That was against my better judgement, I tried to avoid it but I was overridden.'

(2011)

Interviewer Alan Titchmarsh:

'This year you were awarded The Oldie *magazine's Oldie of the Year Award...'*

Philip: *'Well, so what? You just get old.'*

(2011)

Early on in their marriage Princess Elizabeth and Philip were crossing the water to Vancouver Island in Canada.

In bad weather the ship rocked violently and a young petty officer dropped a tray of tea cakes.

Philip got down on his knees and retrieved a handful of cakes, telling his new wife,

'I've got mine – yours are down there!'

'My job, first, second and last is never to let the Queen down.'

Told to his first Private Secretary Michael Parker in the 1950s.

Named as the Oldie of the Year he wrote to the magazine:

'I much appreciate your invitation to receive an "Oldie of the Year Award".

'There is nothing like it for morale to be reminded that the years are passing – ever more quickly – and that bits are beginning to drop off the ancient frame. But it is nice to be remembered at all.

'I regret not being able to receive the award in person, but I will not be conveniently in reach of London at the time.

'I hope the party at Simpsons will be a great success.'

(2011)

Interviewer Fiammetta Rocco asked the Prince about rumours that he had had several affairs during his marriage.

He replied:

'Good God woman, I don't know what sort of company you keep. Have you ever stopped to think that for the last forty years I have never moved anywhere without a policeman accompanying me? So how the hell could I ever get away with anything like that?'

(1993)

He once told a friend:

'How could I be unfaithful to the Queen? There is no way she could possibly retaliate.'

On the Monarchy:

'We are not a secret society.'

Just before Princess Diana's funeral, Princes William and Harry were reluctant to walk behind their mother's coffin.

Philip told them:

'When you are older you might regret not doing so.

'So if I walk, will you walk with me?'

(1997)

'You have to make compromises – that's life.'

(1999)

'I don't think I think very much about "fun".'

(1999)

Asked by a teenager if, on his travels, he was ever nervous at meeting Heads of State:

'Well, it's surprising how you grow out of it!'

(1965)

After Prince William was filmed cleaning a loo on his gap year in Chile, Philip remarked:

'The more accessible you become, the more ordinary you become. The argument could be that if you are ordinary, what are you doing anyway?

(2000)

He once explained that there were few career options for his children.

'They could go into the church, but any commercial or competitive activity is always criticised,' he said.

'I never see any home cooking – all I get is fancy stuff.'

(1962)

During a performance of *Betty Blue Eyes,* Philip saw both himself and the Queen portrayed by actors.

Afterwards he met Annalisa Rossi, who played the Queen, and told her:

'You remind me of somebody...'

He then told Dan Burton, who played the Duke in 1947:

'I like the hair.'

(2011)

'It's the secret of a happy marriage to have different interests.'

(2006)

'I don't have opinions about things I know nothing about.'

(2006)

To the Queen after her Coronation:

'Where did you get that hat?'

(1953)

As the Queen struggled to slice through a fruit cake with thick icing made to celebrate the 250th anniversary of the royal gardens at Kew, Philip told her:

'Press down harder!'

(2009)

To a group of students in the 1980s:

'I am one of those stupid bums that never went to university – and a fat lot of harm it did me.'

Asked how he relaxes he replied:

'Have dinner and go to bed.'

(2006)

In the 1980s Ben Rosen, then chairman of Compaq Computers, hosted a lunch for Philip but couldn't tear him away from the general manager's wife.

He said: *'From the moment we were seated the Prince spoke exclusively to her and neither I nor anyone else at the table could get a word in edgewise, and I was the host!'*

Eventually there was a break and Mr Rosen asked the Prince:

'Your Royal Highness I understand you still fly airplanes.'

There was an embarrassing silence before Philip stared witheringly at him and replied:

'Yes, you know I am in that STILL period of my life. That period when I can STILL lift a fork [he lifted a fork] *STILL lift a glass* [lifted a glass] *and STILL breathe.*

'Yes, I can STILL fly!'

Mr Rosen said afterwards, *'With that he turned away from me and returned to his conversation with the manager's wife. I, on the other hand, crawled under the table.'*

'It is a complete misconception to imagine that the monarchy exists in the interest of the monarch. It doesn't. It exists in the interests of the people.

'If at any time any nation decides that the system is unacceptable, then it is up to them to change it.'

Canadian speech.

(1969)

After the death of the Queen Mother, courtiers floated the idea of Philip being elevated to a knight of the Royal Victorian Order.

He rejected the offer saying the honour was *'an order for servants.'*

(2002)

At a celebration to mark his 87th birthday Philip was seated next to former BP chief Lord Browne who had attracted headlines about his private life.

'I gather you've had some problems since we last met,' said the Prince.

'Don't worry, there's a lot of that in my family.'

(2008)

In an interview with Gyles Brandreth he was asked:

'How do you think you are seen?'

He replied: *'I don't know. Refugee husband I suppose.'*

(1999)

Asked about countries he still hadn't been to and would like to visit:

'If I name them, they might invite me and then, if I couldn't make it, there'd be trouble.'

(1999)

'I thought I was going to have a career in the Navy, but it became obvious there was no hope.

'The Royal Family then [1947] was just the King and Queen and the two princesses. The only other male was the Duke of Gloucester. There was no choice.'

(1999)

'The first ten years (after marrying) I don't remember much about.'

(1999)

'I don't think I have ever got up to make a speech of any kind, anywhere, ever, and not made the audience laugh at least once.'

(1999)

'I take an interest in comparative religion, but if I talk about it I'm labelled a crank.'

(1999)

'I suppose I challenge things to stimulate myself and to be stimulating. 'You don't have to agree with everyone all the time.'

(1999)

'I've become a caricature. There we are. I've just got to live with it.'

(1999)

'I suppose there are a few fortunate souls who have managed to get through life without any anxieties, but my experience is that life has its ups and downs – for most of us anyway.'

(2001)

On his time in the Navy:

'I don't think I ever thought of the sea as something to like.

'It's cold and wet. Sometimes it looks spectacular and you see wonderful sights – though after four years on the morning watch I got fed up with the sunrise.

'I can tell you, there are moments when the sea is bloody.

'Sometimes you feel this is the only sort of life and ten minutes later you're praying for death.'

At a champagne reception in Windsor Castle to celebrate his 80th birthday the Queen told him:

'I can't believe you're 80!'

Philip said: *'I'm not sure that I recommend being 80. It's not so much the age, but trying to survive these celebrations!'*

(2001)

'Every time I talk to a woman they say I've been to bed with her.

'Well I'm bloody flattered at my age to think some pretty girl is interested in me.'

(2006)

In an interview with royal biographer Douglas Keay for *Saga* magazine, Philip said:

'It's much better to go when you are still capable than wait until people say you're so doddery it's time you went.'

When Keay said it was different for the Duke, Philip asked: *'Why?'*

'Well, the fact is that the Queen is not going to abdicate.'

'Who said that?' said Philip, mischievously.

(1999)

To celebrate his 90th birthday, Philip was given a pair of ear defenders for when he goes shooting by the Royal National Institute for the Deaf, now re-named Action on Hearing Loss.

As he was presented with them at a Buckingham Palace reception, he said:

'Can you get Radio Three on these?'

(2011)

Asked if he had been a successful consort he replied:

'I couldn't care less.

'Who cares what I think. I mean it's ridiculous.'

(2011)

Talking about his childhood:

'If anything, I've thought of myself as Scandinavian, particularly Danish. We spoke English at home.

'The others learned Greek. I could understand a certain amount of it.

'But then the conversation would go into French, then it went into German on occasions because we had German cousins.

'If you couldn't think of a word in one language, you tended to go off in another.'

(1992)

Interviewed by Alan Titchmarsh he was asked: *'When you look back, is there anything you would have done differently?'*

Philip replied:

'Well, yes, I would rather have not made the mistakes I did make, but I'm not telling you what they were.'

(2011)

Years after he first met the young Princess Elizabeth, he told his wife:

'You were so shy. I couldn't get a word out of you.'

According to royal author Philip Eade the Prince realised at a young age that he was sometimes rude to people and tried to explain himself in a letter to an aunt. He wrote:

'I am rude and I say many things out of turn.

'Then I am full with remorse and try to get things right.

'I can only assume that it is largely due to the accumulation of toasts to my health over the years that I am still enjoying a fairly satisfactory state of health and have reached such an unexpectedly great age.'

To a Guildhall lunch in the City of London to celebrate his 80th birthday.

(2001)

On a visit to Harrow the Duke was invited to take part in a football training session by local coach Mo Kassamali.

He declined the offer saying:

'The old heart's not working.'

(2012)

Talking about being consort to the Queen, Philip revealed how in the early days he struggled to find a role for himself.

'The problem was of course to recognise what the niche was and to try and grow into it and that was by trial and error.

'There was no precedent.

'If I asked somebody, "what do you expect me to do?" they all looked blank.

'They had no idea, nobody had much idea.'

(2011)

'You don't really want nonagenarians as heads of organisations which are trying to do something useful.'

'There is an ageism in this country, as everywhere, and quite rightly so, because I think you go downhill – physically, mentally and everything.'

'It's better to get out before you reach the sell-by date.'

(2011)

'I reckon I've done my bit. I want to enjoy myself for a bit now.'

'With less responsibility, less rushing about, less preparation, less trying to think of something to say.'

'On top of that your memory's going.'

'I can't remember names.'

'Yes, I'm just sort of winding down.'

(2011)